CONTENTS

KT-438-473

WHAT IS A SUPERCAR?

A supercar is a sports car that is very powerful and very fast. Supercars are production cars, but they are made in very small numbers. They are built using the cutting-edge technology found in racing cars, and are very expensive, often costing more than £1 million.

HUGE POWER
*The Koenigsegg One:1 has an incredible one **hp** of power for every kg of weight.*

FAMOUS COLLECTORS
Supercars are often bought by collectors who have many different cars. Prince Rainer III of Monaco (1923–2005) assembled a huge collection of cars during his lifetime, including several supercars. They are now on display in a museum in Monaco.

A 1995 Ferrari F50 GT at the Monaco Top Cars Collection Museum, which displays the car collection of Prince Rainer III.

MOTORMANIA

SUPER CARS

ROB COLSON

First published in Great Britain
in 2020 by Wayland
Copyright © Hodder and Stoughton, 2020
All rights reserved

Series editor: John Hort
Produced by Tall Tree Ltd
Designer: Jonathan Vipond

HB ISBN: 978 1 5263 1308 9
PB ISBN: 978 1 5263 1309 6

Wayland
An imprint of Hachette Children's Group
Part of Hodder and Stoughton
Carmelite House
50 Victoria Embankment
London EC4Y 0DZ

An Hachette UK Company
www.hachette.co.uk
www.hachettechildrens.co.uk

Printed and bound in China

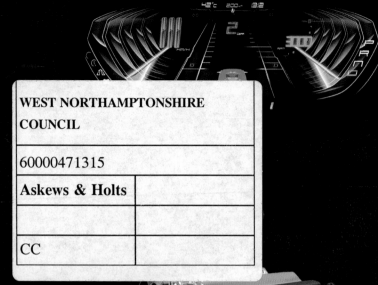

Picture Credits
t-top, b-bottom, l-left, r-right, c-centre, fc-front cover,
bc-back cover

fc, 27t dimcars/Shutterstock.com, bc, 26–27 VanderWolf
Images/Shutterstock.com, 1, 12–13 Bugatti Automobiles, 2t, 21t
W Motors, 2c, 12b Florian Lindner, 2b, 24–25, 24b Igor Karasi/
Shutterstock.com, 3tr, 18–19, 19b Christopher Lyzcen/
Shutterstock.com, 3b, 27b Zavatskiy Aleksandr/Shutterstock.
com, 4–5 Dong liu/Shutterstock.com, 4b Dmitry Eagle Orlov/
Shutterstock.com, 5t Max Earey/Shutterstock.com, 6–7, 7t, 7c, 7b
Lamborghini SpA, 8–9 BMW AG, 8b Lothar Spurzem, 9b
nakhon100, 10–11t, 10–11b, 11tr, 11c McLaren Automotive, 13t
Skoda Auto, 13b Supermac1961, 14–15, 14b, 15t, 15b Lexus, 16,
17c Roland Woon/Shutterstock.com, 17t Nic Redhead, 17b
Axion23, 18b, 19t Gustavo Fadel/Shutterstock.com, 19b Mark
Thompson/Getty Images, 20bl, 21c slava296/Shutterstock.com,
20–21 M7kk/Shutterstock.com, 21b Schitzique, 22–23, 22b, 23c,
23bl, 23b4 Porsche AG, 25t supergenijalac/Shutterstock.com,
27c Koenigsegg, 28t, 28b, 29t, 29c, 29b Hennessey Ltd

Every attempt has been made to clear copyright. Should
there be any inadvertent omission, please apply to the
publisher for rectification.

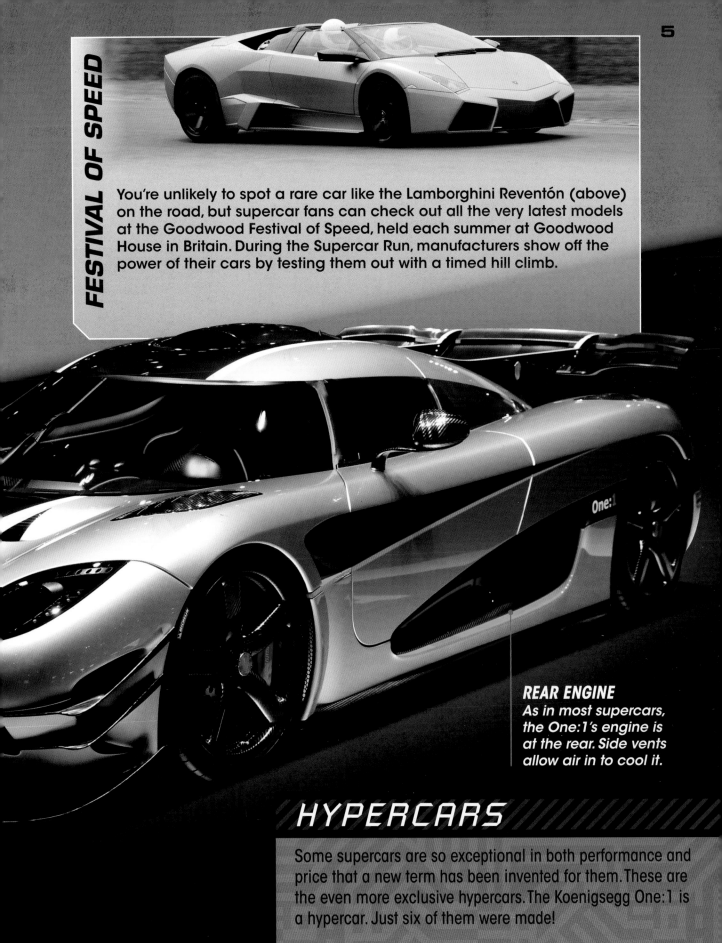

FESTIVAL OF SPEED

You're unlikely to spot a rare car like the Lamborghini Reventón (above) on the road, but supercar fans can check out all the very latest models at the Goodwood Festival of Speed, held each summer at Goodwood House in Britain. During the Supercar Run, manufacturers show off the power of their cars by testing them out with a timed hill climb.

REAR ENGINE
As in most supercars, the One:1's engine is at the rear. Side vents allow air in to cool it.

HYPERCARS

Some supercars are so exceptional in both performance and price that a new term has been invented for them. These are the even more exclusive hypercars. The Koenigsegg One:1 is a hypercar. Just six of them were made!

LAMBORGHINI
MIURA

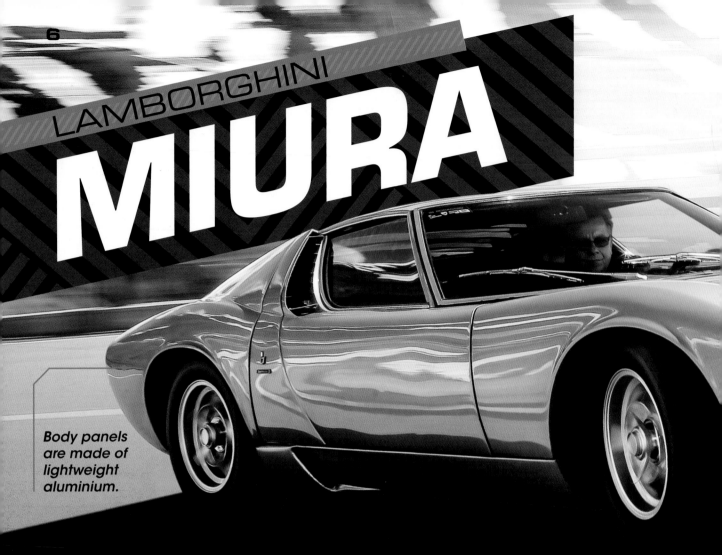

Body panels are made of lightweight aluminium.

The Miura was the first sports car to be thought of as a supercar. With its central V12 engine and streamlined design, it brought a racing car's performance to the road.

MIURA

YEARS OF PRODUCTION:
1966–1973

NUMBER BUILT:
764

PRICE IN 1966:
£10,000
(£120,000 equivalent in 2020)

ENGINE:
3.9 litre, 12 **cylinders**

POWER:
350 hp

TOP SPEED:
280 km/h

0–100 KM/H:
6.7 seconds

SECRET PROJECT

The Miura was developed in 1965 by three of Lamborghini's senior engineers in their spare time. They had trouble convincing their boss, Ferruccio Lamborghini, that there was a market for such an expensive car. By the time the **prototype** was shown at the 1966 Geneva Motor Show, Lamborghini had been won over. It entered production soon after.

'278472 C'A'

The headlights have distinctive 'eyelashes'.

GIAN PAOLO DALLARA

Lamborghini's first chief car designer, Gian Paolo Dallara (born 1936), worked on the **chassis** design of the Miura, and helped to establish the company as a leader in high-performance road cars. Later, he turned to racing cars, setting up his own company, Dallara Automobili, in 1972.

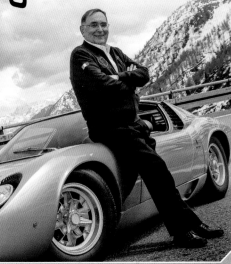

CHANGING GEAR

*The Miura was fitted with a five-speed manual **gearbox**, operated by a leather gear stick.*

MID-ENGINED CAR

The Miura was the first high-performance sports car to have a mid-engined, two-seater layout. Moving the engine from the front of the car places more weight on the rear wheels. This helps the car to grip the road when accelerating or taking corners. It is now the standard design for nearly all supercars.

BMW
M1

Developed in collaboration with Lamborghini, the M1 was BMW's first mid-engine car. It was produced for racing, but 400 road-going models were made in order to meet the requirements to enter the car for touring car race categories.

The body was made from lightweight fibreglass.

RACING SERIES

In 1979 and 1980, BMW ran a racing series in which all drivers used an identical M1 car. The series was a pure test of driving ability and it attracted many of the top Formula 1 stars. The first championship was won by Austrian Nikki Lauda and the second by Brazilian Nelson Piquet, both of whom were also multiple F1 champions.

This is the M1 driven by Nelson Piquet in 1980. For racing, the M1 was fitted with a low front spoiler, wide wheel arches and an adjustable rear wing.

M1

The wheels were made from a specially developed **alloy**.

TECH POINT

The M1 was built around a spaceframe chassis. Designed by Lamborghini, the spaceframe was a strong but light structure made of steel tubing. Many high-performance racing cars are made with a spaceframe, but they are difficult to engineer and require extensive testing.

YEARS OF PRODUCTION:
1978–1981

NUMBER BUILT:
453

PRICE IN 1978:
£40,000 (£200,000 equivalent in 2020)

ENGINE:
3.5 litre, 6 cylinders

POWER:
273 hp

TOP SPEED:
262 km/h

0–100 KM/H:
5.9 seconds

The bodywork, interior, engine, **transmission** and **suspension** were all attached to the tubular spaceframe.

MCLAREN

F1

In 1992, champion Formula 1 team McLaren built their first production car. Using the latest racing technology and knowhow, they created the F1, the fastest road-legal car of its time.

RACING LOOK

The car's layout looks very similar to that of a racing car. The driver sits in the middle, creating a central driving position that maximises the car's stability at high speeds. While it is road-legal, the F1 is built for speed, and at the 1995 24 Hours of Le Mans race, a modified F1 beat purpose-built racing cars to claim the overall title.

The 'butterfly' doors open vertically around a front hinge.

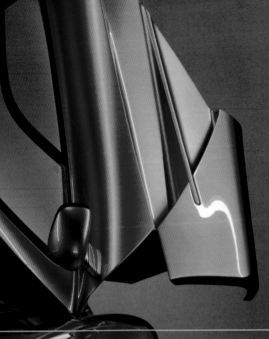

AFTERCARE

Each of the 106 cars was custom built for its owner. While production stopped in 1998, owners can still call upon McLaren engineers who have been specially trained to maintain this model. If necessary, an engineer will fly out to a remote location to fix the car.

F1

YEARS OF PRODUCTION:
1992–1998

NUMBER BUILT:
106

PRICE IN 1992:
£600,000
(£1.2 million equivalent in 2020)

ENGINE:
6.1 litre, 12 cylinders

POWER:
618 hp

0–100 KM/H:
3.7 seconds

TOP SPEED:
350 km/h

The car holds three people. The driver sits in the middle, with one passenger on either side.

Moulded monocoque is light but very strong.

TECH POINT

McLaren used Formula 1 technology to create a light but incredibly strong **monocoque** chassis/body for the F1. The chassis and body are created from one piece of moulded carbon-composite rather than body panels attached to a frame. This saves weight and also allows the car to be moulded into an **aerodynamic** and stylish shape. In this way, McLaren engineers were able to hit the target weight of just 1,018 kg, maximising the car's top speed.

BUGATTI
VEYRON

Designed and engineered by German company Volkswagen and built by French manufacturer Bugatti, the Veyron took over the mantle of fastest production car from the McLaren F1 in 2005. With a huge engine and sturdy body, the Veyron is large, loud and extremely powerful.

HUGE ENGINE

Bugattis are the only production cars in the world to feature a W16 engine, in which 16 cylinders are arranged in a 'W' shape. Turbochargers force compressed air into the engine to keep it running efficiently. At top speed, the engine needs 45,000 litres of air per minute to burn enough fuel. That's as much air as a human breathes in four days. At full throttle, it burns a litre of fuel every 10 seconds.

Four turbochargers force air into the 16 cylinders.

Slovak designer Josef Kaban (born 1973) was a rising young star at Volkswagen when he designed the exterior of the Bugatti Veyron. He later worked for Audi and Skoda, and is now Head Designer at BMW.

The aluminium front grille allows air into the radiator.

VEYRON

YEARS OF PRODUCTION:
2005–2015

NUMBER BUILT:
450

PRICE:
£1.5 million

ENGINE:
8 litre, 16 cylinders

POWER:
987 hp (standard version)

0–100 KM/H:
2.46 seconds

TOP SPEED:
408 km/h

SUPER SPORT

In 2010, Bugatti brought out a limited edition of the Veyron called the Super Sport. By adding larger turbochargers, Bugatti's engineers managed to increase the power to 1,200 hp, and the Super Sport was recorded on the track at a record-breaking top speed of 431 km/h. On the road, it is limited to 415 km/h to protect the tyres from wear.

BD·928·QB

LEXUS LFA

Lexus, the luxury car division of Japanese manufacturer Toyota, released its first supercar in 2010. The LFA may not be the fastest supercar ever made, but thanks to its smooth engine, it is one of the most pleasurable to drive.

Unlike most supercars, the engine is placed just in front of the driver.

Bumpers are made from reinforced panels.

NÜRBURGRING PACKAGE

*Fifty of the 500 LFAs were made in a special racing 'Nürburgring package'. With 10 mm lower suspension, an added rear wing and side spoilers, they were designed to provide extra **downforce** at high speed. This makes for a less comfortable ride, but is perfect for owners to test their car on the track.*

HIGH-TECH BODY

To make the body of the LFA, Lexus borrowed the latest aerospace technology. Two-thirds of the body was made from **carbon fibre-reinforced plastic (CFRP)**, and a third from aluminium. The carbon fibres were woven together in specially made high-tech looms.

The CFRP used in the body is lighter than aluminium, but four times stronger.

Side air intakes cool the brakes and the rear radiator.

LFA

YEARS OF PRODUCTION:
2010–2012

NUMBER BUILT:
500

PRICE:
£300,000

ENGINE:
4.8 litre, 10 cylinders

POWER:
553 hp

TOP SPEED:
298 km/h

0–100 KM/H:
3.7 seconds

TECH POINT

Lexus developed the roaring **V10** engine especially for the LFA. With slightly smaller cylinders than a **V8** engine of the same size, it can operate at up to **9,000 revolutions per minute (rpm)**. This high rpm gives the engine a fast response time. It can move from zero to maximum rpm in just over half a second.

PAGANI
HUAYRA

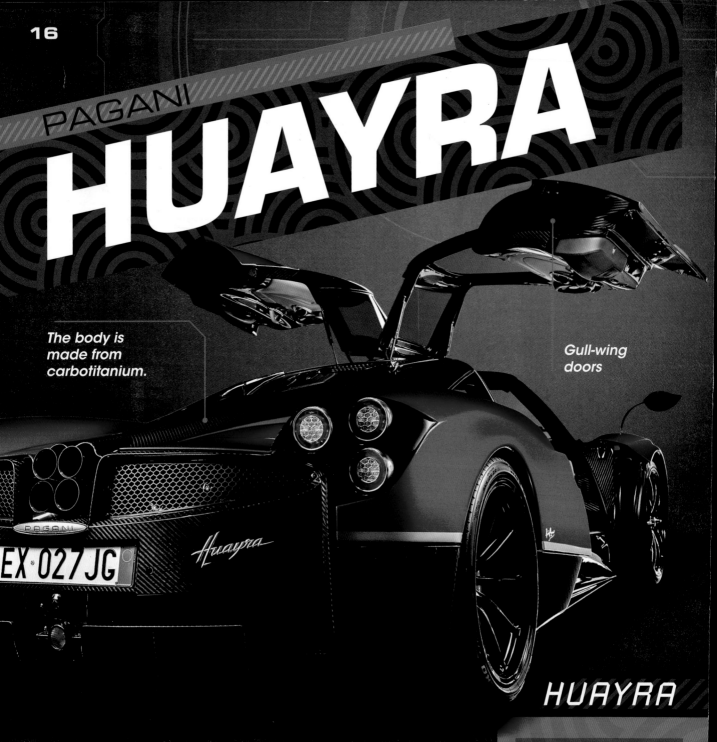

The body is made from carbotitanium.

Gull-wing doors

HUAYRA

YEARS OF PRODUCTION:
2012–2018

NUMBER BUILT:
100

PRICE:
£1 million

Italian manufacturer Pagani teamed up with engine-supplier Mercedes-AMG to produce the Huayra. It is named after an ancient Inca god of the wind, and its sleek, aerodynamic shape was inspired by the wing of an aircraft.

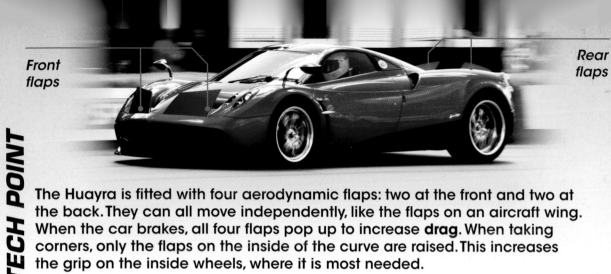

Front flaps

Rear flaps

The Huayra is fitted with four aerodynamic flaps: two at the front and two at the back. They can all move independently, like the flaps on an aircraft wing. When the car brakes, all four flaps pop up to increase **drag**. When taking corners, only the flaps on the inside of the curve are raised. This increases the grip on the inside wheels, where it is most needed.

Leaf-shaped wing mirrors on carbon-fibre 'stalks'

EVELOPING THE DESIGN

Huayra spent nearly ten years in development,
Pagani engineers strove to create a car that
uld give the driver the feeling of brute force
nerated by an airplane at take-off. To produce
acceleration needed, the car had to be both
werful and as light as possible. Pagani tested
ht scale models and two full-size models
ore finalising the design.

SPECIAL EDITIONS
Several customers have ordered specially made one-off versions of the Huayra. These include the Carbon Edition (below), which has a body and wheels made entirely from carbon fibre, and the Huayra Pearl, which has a more powerful engine and lighter weight.

OP SPEED:

3 km/h

NGINE:

itre, 12 cylinders

OWER:

0 hp

-100 KM/H:

7 seconds

FERRARI LAFERRARI

The LaFerrari is the most powerful supercar Italian manufacturer Ferrari has ever produced. It is a hybrid, meaning that its large petrol engine can have its power boosted by an electric motor.

LAFERRARI

YEARS OF PRODUCTION:
2013–2016

NUMBER MADE:
499

PRICE:
£1.2 million

ENGINE:
6.3 litre, 12 cylinders

POWER:
949 hp

TOP SPEED:
Over 350 km/h

0–100 KM/H:
2.4 seconds

Large side air intakes

HIGH-TECH BRAKES
The LaFerrari is fitted with brake discs made from a mix of carbon fibres and ceramic. The mixture was developed by Italian brake specialists Brembo. The discs create less heat than conventional metal brake discs and also save weight.

HYBRID ENGINE

The car is powered primarily by the engine, but the electric motor can give short bursts of extra power when it accelerates. The motor's battery contains 120 high-voltage cells, which are charged by recovering energy when the car brakes. The cells are also charged by the engine whenever it is producing more turning force, or **torque**, than is needed to turn the wheels, such as when it is taking corners.

The engine is kept cool by a system of water pipes.

Wide, low bonnet

RACING KNOWHOW

The engineers who designed the LaFerrari drew on the experience of legendary F1 racing car designer Rory Byrne (born 1944) to produce a structure that combined minimum weight, which is good for speed, with maximum rigidity, which is good for handling. In his years as Ferrari's chief designer, Byrne designed 11 different cars, winning 99 Grands Prix and 7 constructors' titles.

LYKAN
HYPERSPORT

Designed by Lebanese engineers and built in Dubai by W Motors, the Lykan Hypersport is the first sports car to be designed and made in the Middle East. With just seven cars made in total, it is one of the most exclusive supercars ever produced.

Sharply angled windscreen

Rectangular exhaust pipes

PRECIOUS JEWELS

The Lykan Hypersport is the ultimate vehicle of luxurious excess. The headlights are encrusted with 440 diamonds, and customers could add rubies and sapphires to change their colour.

TECH POINT

In the centre of the car, next to the driver, is a 3D holographic display console. It is interactive, allowing the driver to operate the **GPS** navigation system or change the music with just a wave of the hand.

HYPERSPORT

YEARS OF PRODUCTION:
2013–2016

NUMBER BUILT:
7

PRICE:
£2.7 million

ENGINE:
3.7 litre, 6 cylinders

POWER:
781 hp

TOP SPEED:
395 km/h

0–100 KM/H:
2.9 seconds

POLICE CAR
The Abu Dhabi police force bought a Lykan Hypersport in 2015. It became fully operational four years later, fitted with flashing lights that somewhat spoil the car's aerodynamic design.

PORSCHE
918 SPYDER

The 918 Spyder is a high-performance hybrid sports car, powered by a petrol engine and two electric motors. It can run on just the engine when out on the open road, or it can glide silently and emission-free using only the electric motors in the city.

TECH POINT

The car is shaped to allow air to flow over, under and through it as aerodynamically as possible. It is fitted with an active aerodynamic system made up of the rear wing, flaps in the underbody and air intakes under the headlights. These are constantly adjusted to ensure best performance.

The underbody is fully enclosed so that air flows smoothly under the car.

RACING BALANCE

The design of the 918 Spyder was inspired by racing technology. Its monocoque chassis is made from weight-saving carbon fibre-reinforced plastic, while the heavier components, including the engine and battery, are placed as centrally and deeply as possible. This creates a very low centre of gravity, with slightly more weight towards the rear of the car, which helps it to grip the road when cornering at high speeds.

918 SPYDER

YEARS OF PRODUCTION:
2013–2015

NUMBER BUILT:
918

PRICE:
£670,000

ENGINE:
4.6 litre, 8 cylinders, plus two electric motors

POWER:
887 hp

TOP SPEED:
340 km/h

0–100 KM/H:
2.9 seconds

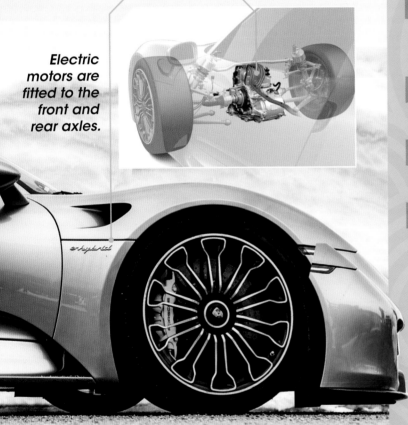

Electric motors are fitted to the front and rear axles.

TRACK RECORD

In 2013, Porsche demonstrated the speed and agility of the 918 Spyder by testing out a racing version on the Nürburgring track in Germany. It completed one lap of the 20.6-kilometre circuit in 6 minutes, 57 seconds, becoming the first road-legal car to break the 7-minute barrier.

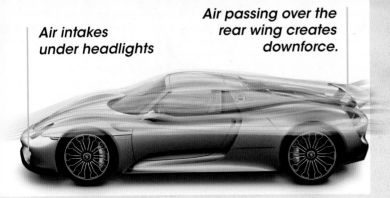

Air intakes under headlights

Air passing over the rear wing creates downforce.

RIMAC
CONCEPT ONE

The Concept One, made in Croatia by Rimac Automobili, is the world's first all-electric supercar. As powerful as a Bugatti Veyron, it was the fastest-accelerating electric vehicle ever made when it first came out.

CONTROLLED POWER

With a separate motor turning each wheel, the car can switch from front-wheel drive to rear-wheel drive or four-wheel drive, depending on the driving conditions. Rimac designed and built the electrical systems needed for the precise control of high-performance cars from scratch, taking out 24 patents on new technologies along the way.

MATE RIMAC

Croatian engineer Mate Rimac started converting petrol cars into electric ones as a hobby. He won races driving his converted electric cars, and this attracted the attention of investors. With the money in place, he founded Rimac Automobili in 2009 to pursue his ambition to create the first electric high-performance car.

ONGOING DEVELOPMENT

The first Concept One was completed in 2013, but Rimac continued to develop the car and presented a more powerful version at the 2016 Geneva Motor Show. A year later, it broke the lap record for an electric car at the Goodwood race track in England. In 2017, its range on one charge was increased to 350 kilometres. Eventually, Rimac hope to give their cars a range of more than 500 kilometres.

CONCEPT ONE

YEARS OF PRODUCTION:
2013–

NUMBER BUILT:
88 planned

PRICE:
£800,000

MOTORS:
4 electric motors, powered by a 90 kWh battery

POWER:
1,224 hp

TOP SPEED:
395 km/h

0–100 KM/H:
2.4 seconds

KOENIGSEGG
AGERA RS

The Agera RS was declared the fastest production car ever when it was tested in 2015. Although it is completely road-legal, it contains many features designed for optimum performance on the track.

The low front spoiler creates downforce.

AGERA RS

YEARS OF PRODUCTION:
2015–2018

NUMBER BUILT:
25

POWER:
1,160 hp

PRICE:
£2 million

TOP SPEED:
458 km/h

ENGINE:
5 litre, 8 cylinders

0–100 KM/H:
2.9 seconds

ACTIVE WING

The rear wing changes angle automatically as the car moves. When the brakes are applied, it points up at 25 degrees, an angle that produces both drag to slow the car down and downforce to keep it on the road. At high speeds, it lies almost flat to minimise drag.

The wing is operated by lightweight carbon rods.

CHRISTIAN KOENIGSEGG

Koenigsegg was founded in Sweden in 1994 by 22-year-old engineer Christian von Koenigsegg. Eight years later, the company produced its first street-legal production car, the CCX. It has since won a reputation for innovation – developing and building its own components. The company has a large engineering department of 25 engineers, led by von Koenigsegg.

The body is made of lightweight carbon fibre.

HOLLOW WHEELS

Koenigsegg were the first manufacturer to fit production cars with carbon fibre wheels. The Agera's 'Aircore' wheels are each made from one piece of light carbon fibre. They are hollow, saving about 20 kg in weight.

HENNESSEY
VENOM F5

US company Hennessey took the Venom F5 into production in 2019 with the aim of making the fastest road-legal car ever. The F5 is named after the highest rating on the Fujita scale for tornadoes.

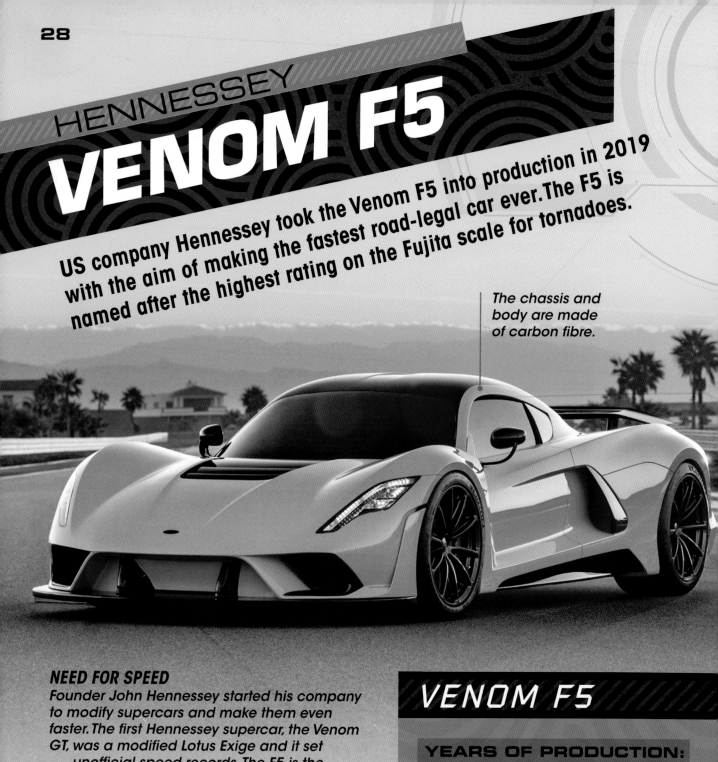

The chassis and body are made of carbon fibre.

NEED FOR SPEED

Founder John Hennessey started his company to modify supercars and make them even faster. The first Hennessey supercar, the Venom GT, was a modified Lotus Exige and it set unofficial speed records. The F5 is the first car Hennessey will have built from scratch, and the goal is to take the official record this time.

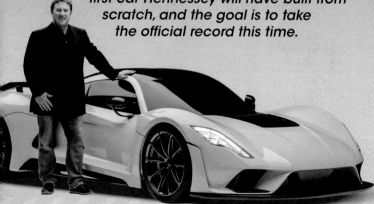

VENOM F5

YEARS OF PRODUCTION:
2019–

NUMBER BUILT:
Planned to be 24

PRICE:
£1.2 million

ENGINE:
7.6 litre, 8 cylinders

TECH POINT

The key to the F5's speed is its huge 7.6-litre engine. The cars customers will buy will be limited to 1,600 hp for safety reasons, but Hennessey say they have tested the engine at over 2,000 hp, and it held together!

Two huge turbochargers boost the engine's power.

FASTER THAN F1

With the Venom F5, Hennessey intends to create the supercar with the fastest acceleration ever. They expect the car to be capable reaching 300 km/h from a standing start in less than 10 seconds – that's faster than a Formula 1 car.

The rear wing lowers when the car accelerates to improve its aerodynamics.

POWER:
Restricted to 1,600 hp

TOP SPEED:
Intended to be over 484 km/h

0–100 KM/H:
Predicted to be under 2.5 seconds

GLOSSARY

Aerodynamic
Describes an object that is shaped in a way that allows air to move smoothly around it when it moves.

Alloy
A material made by mixing two or more metals or by mixing metal with other substances.

Carbon fibre
A strong but lightweight material made from very thin threads of carbon that have been woven together.

Chassis
A strong frame to which the body of a car is attached.

Cylinders
The parts of an engine inside which fuel burns to pump pistons and generate power.

Downforce
A force that pushes down on a car to keep it on the road. Parts of a car are designed to generate the right amount of downforce without producing too much drag.

Drag
A force that resists the movement of an object passing through a gas or liquid.

Fibreglass
A light but strong material made of plastic reinforced by glass fibres.

Gearbox
The system of gears in a car. Gears change the speed at which the engine's power drives the wheels.

GPS
Short for 'Global Positioning System', a navigation system that works by communicating with satellites.

Horsepower (hp)
A unit of measurement for power, or the rate at which work is done. One horsepower is roughly equal to the power of one strong horse.

Monocoque
A strong exterior shell of a vehicle that provides it with structural support.

Prototype
A model of a new vehicle that is made to test the design.

Revolutions per minute (rpm)
A measure of the speed of an engine, counting turns of the crankshaft in one minute.

Spoiler
A part on a car designed to create downforce by increasing drag.

Suspension
A system of springs and shock absorbers that attach the wheels to a car's chassis.

Torque
A measure of the force that makes an object, such as a wheel, rotate around an axis.

Transmission
The part of a car that transfers power from the engine to the wheels via a gearbox.